My Pony Logbook

A Personal Record of My Pony

ILLUSTRATED BY JENNIFER BELL

British Library Cataloguing-in-Publication Data.
A catalogue record for this book is available from the British Library

ISBN 0 85131 865 7

© Concept/text J. A. Allen, an imprint of Robert Hale Ltd. 2002
© (illustrations) Jennifer Bell 2002

No part of this book may be reproduced, stored in a
retrieval system, or transmitted, in any form or by any
means, electronic, mechanical, photocopying,
recording or otherwise, without the prior permission
of the publisher. All rights reserved.

Published in Great Britain in 2002 by
J. A. Allen, an imprint of Robert Hale Ltd.,
Clerkenwell House, 45–47 Clerkenwell Green,
London EC1R 0HT
Reprinted 2004
Reprinted 2005

Illustrated by Jennifer Bell
Design by Paul Saunders

Colour processing by Tenon & Polert Colour Processing Ltd., Hong Kong
Printed in China by Midas Printing International Ltd.

Contents

My Personal Notes 4
My Pony 5
My Pony's Vital Statistics 6
My Pony's Insurance 7
My Pony Lives 8
My Pony's Blacksmith 10
My Pony's Shoeing Record 12
My Pony's Vet 15
My Pony's Veterinary Record 16
My Pony's First Aid Box 19
My Pony's Grooming Kit 20
My Pony's Diet 22
My Pony's Worming Record 23
My Pony's Tack 26
My Pony's Saddle 27
My Pony's Stable Clothing 29
My Road Safety Wear 32
My Riding Clothes 33
My Riding School 36
My Lunge Lesson 37
My Jumping Lesson 38

My First Fall 39
My Schooling Programme 40
My Riding Lesson Record 41
My Riding Friends 44
My Favourite Ride 45
My Pony's First Gymkhana 47
My Pony's Best Performance 48
My Pony's First Rosette 49
Our First Rosette 50
Show and Gymkhana Record 51
My Pony's First Showing
   Class 55
My Pony's First Dressage
   Competition 56
My Pony's First Jumping
   Competition 57
My Pony's First Hunter Trial 58
My Best Moment 59
My Worst Moment 60
My Riding Ambitions 61
My Special Memories 62

My Personal Notes

This pony logbook belongs to ―――――――――

――――――――――――――――――――

My address is ―――――――――――――――

――――――――――――――――――――

―――――――――――――――――

My telephone number is

Home ――――――――――

Mobile ――――――――――

In case of emergency

Contact ――――――――――

―――――――――――――――

―――――――――――――――

Telephone ――――――――――

―――――――――――――――

My Pony

Stick a photograph of your pony here

My pony's name is _____

_____

My Pony's Vital Statistics

Breed _____

Colour _____

Markings _____
_____

Height _____ Age _____

Sire _____

Dam _____

Purchased from _____

_____

_____

Date of purchase

_____

_____

_____

My Pony's Insurance

Insurance company _____

_____

Policy number _____

Type of cover _____

_____

Renewal date _____

Freeze, brand, or other identification mark details

_____

_____

My Pony Lives

Stable address ─────────────────────

─────────────────────────────────

Description of paddock ──────────────

─────────────────────────────────

─────────────────────────────────

─────────────────────────────────

─────────────────────────────────

My pony's equine companions are _____

My Pony's Blacksmith

Name _____

Address _____

_____

_____

Home telephone _____

Mobile _____

Fax _____

e-mail _____

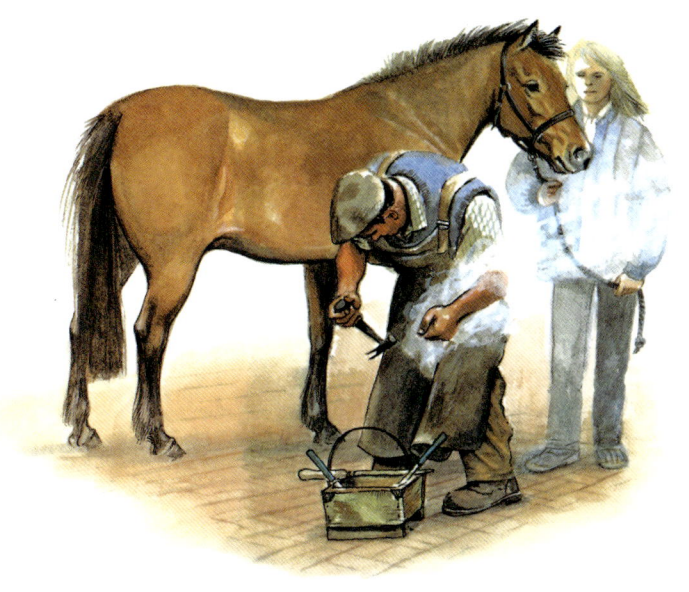

Type of shoe _____

_____

Size of shoe _____

My Pony's Shoeing Record

Date _____

Details _____

_____

Date _____

Details _____

_____

Date _____

Details _____

_____

Date _____

Details _____

_____

_____

_____

Date _____

Details _____

_____

Date _____

Details _____

_____

Date _____

Details _____

_____

Date _____

Details _____

_____

Date _____

Details _____

_____

Date _____

Details _____

_____

Date _____

Details _____

_____

My Pony's Vet

Name _____

_____

Practice address _____

_____

_____

Telephone _____

Fax _____

e-mail _____

My Pony's Veterinary Record

Date of visit _____

Ailment/injury _____

Treatment _____

_____

Date of visit _____

Ailment/injury _____

Treatment _____

_____

Date of visit _____

Ailment/injury _____

Treatment _____

_____

_____

_____

Date of visit _____

Ailment/injury _____

Treatment _____

_____

Date of visit _____

Ailment/injury _____

Treatment _____

_____

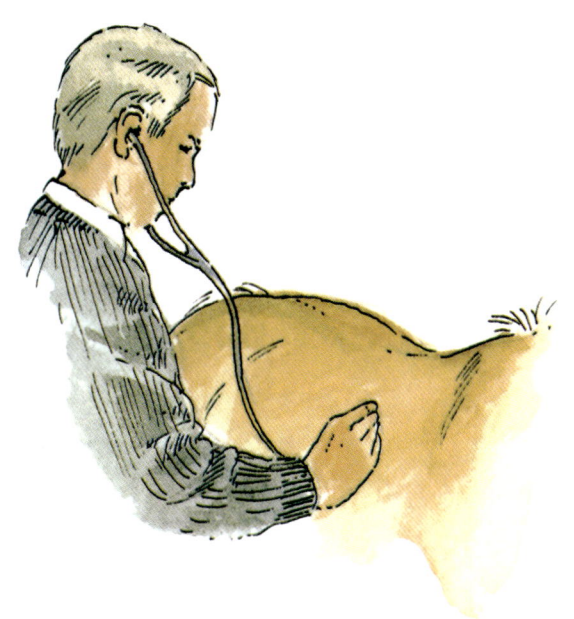

Date of visit _____

Ailment/injury _____

Treatment _____

_____

Date of visit _____

Ailment/injury _____

Treatment _____

_____

My Pony's First Aid Box

First aid items ———————————————

———————————————————————

———————————————————————

———————————————————————

———————————————————————

———————————————————————

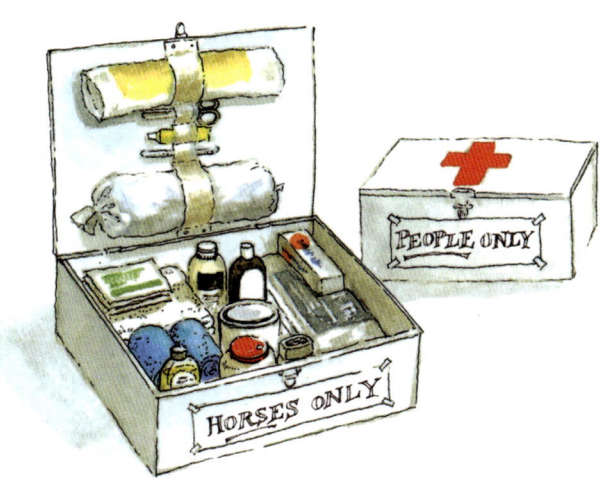

My Pony's Grooming Kit

Grooming equipment ——————————————

My pony's grooming routine

_____

_____

_____

_____

_____

_____

My Pony's Diet

My pony likes ———————————————————

———————————————————

———————————————————

———————————————————

My pony won't eat ——————————————————

———————————————————————————

———————————————————————————

———————————————————————————

My Pony's daily feeding routine

Summer _____

am _____

pm _____

Winter _____

am _____

pm _____

Extras _____

_____

Treats _____

_____

_____

My Pony's Worming Record

Name of wormer ————————————————

Dosage ————————————————

Supplier ————————————————

————————————————

Date of dose ————————————————

Date of dose ————————————————

Date of dose ————————————————

Date of dose ————————————————

Date of dose ————————————————

Date of dose ————————————————

Date of dose ————————————————

Date of dose ————————————————

Date of dose ————————————————

Date of dose ————————————————

Date of dose _____

Date of dose _____

Date of dose _____

Date of dose _____

Date of dose _____

Date of dose _____

Date of dose _____

Date of dose _____

Worming with a syringe

My Pony's Tack

My pony's bridle _____

Size _____

Type of bit _____

Type of metal _____

Type of noseband _____

Type of reins _____

Type of martingale _____

_____

My Pony's Saddle

Type of saddle _____

Make _____

Size _____

Type of stirrups _____

Type of girth _____

Type of numnah _____

Security mark _____

Favourite saddle soap brand _____

Other details _____

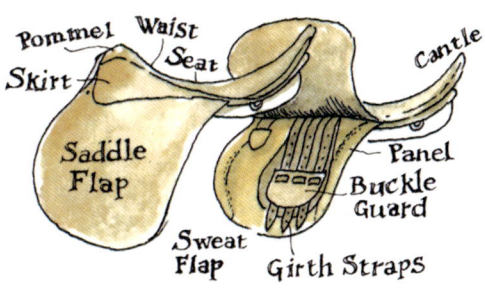

My Pony's Stable Clothing

Type of headcollar rope _____

Colour of headcollar rope _____

Type of night rug _____

Colour _____

Type of surcingle _____

_____

Type of day rug _____

Colour _____

Colour of fly sheet _____

Colour of anti-sweat rug _____

Type of New Zealand rug _____

Colour _____

Colour of tail bandages _____

Colour of leg bandages _____

Details of extra clothing _____

_____

My Road Safety Wear

My pony wears _____

_____

_____

My safety clothing is _____

_____

_____

_____

My Riding Clothes

For casual riding I wear ———————————————

———————————————————————

———————————————————————

———————————————————————

———————————————————————

For shows and gymkhanas I wear _____

For cross country I wear

My Riding School

Name _____

Address _____

_____

My favourite instructor _____

_____

My favourite riding school pony _____

_____

My Lunge Lesson

My instructor _____

Pony _____

_____

Details _____

_____

_____

_____

_____

_____

My Jumping Lesson

My instructor _____

Pony _____

Height jumped _____

Number of refusals _____

Type of obstacles _____

_____

Other details _____

_____

Cross pole

My First Fall

Details _____

_____

_____

_____

_____

_____

_____

My Schooling Programme

Things to improve _____

_____

My riding _____

_____

_____

My pony _____

_____

_____

_____

_____

_____

_____

My Riding Lesson Record

Date _____

Pony _____

Instructor _____

Details _____

_____

Date _____

Pony _____

Instructor _____

Details _____

_____

Date _____

Pony _____

Instructor _____

Details _____

_____

_____

Date _____

Pony _____

Instructor _____

Details _____

_____

_____

Date _____

Pony _____

Instructor _____

Details _____

_____

_____

Date _____

Pony _____

Instructor _____

Details _____

_____

_____

My Riding Friends

Name _____

Home telephone _____

Mobile _____

e-mail _____

Name _____

Home telephone _____

Mobile _____

e-mail _____

Name _____

Home telephone

_____

Mobile _____

_____

e-mail _____

My Favourite Ride

How many miles _____

How long it takes _____

Things to take _____

_____

_____

_____

*Remember! Always tell someone exactly
where you are going!*

Draw a sketch map of your favourite ride

My Pony's First Gymkhana

Location _____

How we got there _____

_____

Classes we entered _____

_____

_____

_____

_____

_____

_____

My Pony's Best Performance

Class _____

Result _____

Details _____

_____

_____

_____

_____

_____

_____

_____

_____

_____

_____

_____

My Pony's First Rosette

Gymkhana _____

Date _____

Class _____

Details _____

_____

_____

Our First Rosette

Photograph of me and my pony with our first rosette

Stick your own photograph on this page

Show and Gymkhana Record

Show _____

Date _____

Classes entered _____

_____

Results _____

_____

_____

Show _____

Date _____

Classes entered _____

_____

Results _____

_____

_____

Show _____

Date _____

Classes entered _____

_____

Results _____

_____

_____

Show _____

Date _____

Classes entered _____

_____

Results _____

_____

Show _____

Date _____

Classes entered _____

_____

Results _____

_____

_____

Show _____

Date _____

Classes entered _____

_____

Results _____

_____

Show _____

Date _____

Classes entered _____

_____

Results _____

_____

_____

Show _____

Date _____

Classes entered _____

_____

Results _____

_____

_____

_____

My Pony's First Showing Class

Date

Show

Class

Result

Details

Our First Dressage Competition

Date _____

Venue _____

Test ridden _____

Marks _____

Details _____

_____

Our First Jumping Competition

Date _____

Venue _____

Class _____

Result _____

Details _____

_____

_____

My Pony's First Hunter Trial

Date

Venue

Result

Details

My Best Moment

Details

My Worst Moment

Details

My Riding Ambitions

My Special Memories

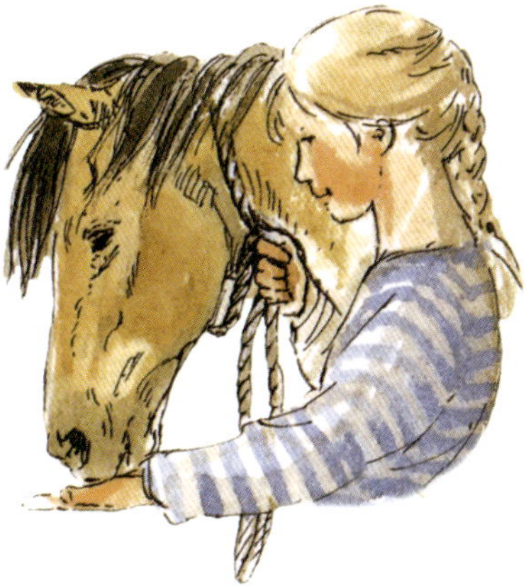

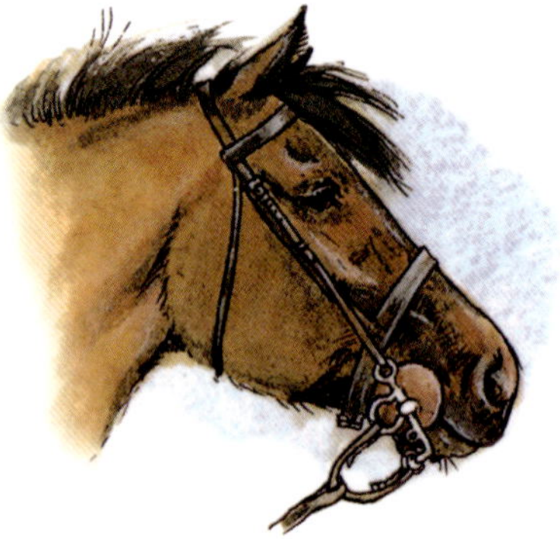